D0005446

STUCK ON SMILES

STUCK ON SMILES

Copyright © 2016 Portable Press

All rights reserved. No part of this publication may be reproduced, distributed, or transmitted in any form or by any means, including photocopying, recording, or other electronic or mechanical methods, without the prior written permission of the publisher, except in the case of brief quotations embodied in critical reviews and certain other noncommercial uses permitted by copyright law.

Portable Press

An imprint of Printers Row Publishing Group

P.O. Box 1117, Ashland, OR 97520

www.bathroomreader.com

e-mail: mail@bathroomreader.com

Printers Row Publishing Group is a division of
Readerlink Distribution Services, LLC.

The Portable Press name and logo is a trademark of
Readerlink Distribution Services, LLC.

All correspondence concerning the content of this book should be addressed to
Portable Press, Editorial Department, at the above address.

Quotes collected and curated by Hannah L. Bingham

Illustrated and designed by Dorit Ely

Portable Press would like to thank the following people
whose advice and assistance made this book possible:

Gordon Javna	**Jay Newman**	**Rusty von Dyl**
Kim T. Griswell	**Melinda Allman**	**Jonathan Lopes**
Trina Janssen	**Jennifer Magee**	**Aaron Guzman**
Brian Boone	**Peter Norton**	

ISBN: 978-1-62686-477-1

Printed in China

First Printing

20 19 18 17 16   1 2 3 4 5

STUCK ON SMILES

QUIRKY GRATITUDE QUOTES
THAT STICK
IN YOUR MEMORY...
AND ON YOUR STUFF.

PORTABLE
PRESS

No one
is useless
in this world
who lightens
the burden
of another.

_____

Charles Dickens

WHEN I STARTED COUNTING MY *blessings* MY WHOLE LIFE *turned around.*

♥

WILLIE NELSON

Some people are always grumbling because roses have thorns;

I am thankful that thorns have roses.

————— ✳ —————

Alphonse Karr

WE DO NOT NEED **MAGIC** TO CHANGE THE WORLD. WE CARRY ALL THE POWER INSIDE OURSELVES ALREADY.

J.K. ROWLING

WHEN YOU COME
TO A ROADBLOCK,
TAKE A
DETOUR.

MARY KAY ASH

WE HOPE THAT,

WHEN THE INSECTS

TAKE OVER THE WORLD,

THEY WILL

REMEMBER

WITH

GRATITUDE

HOW WE TOOK THEM

ALONG ON ALL

OUR PICNICS.

WILLIAM VAUGHN

LIFE HAPPENS

CHOCOLATE HELPS.

BRIGITTE

WHEN
LIFE HANDS YOU
LEMONS, MAKE
A GIN & TONIC.

Colleen Pugh

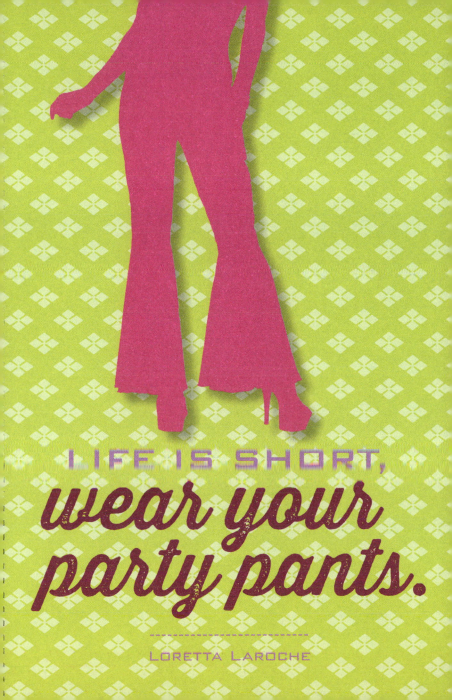

LIFE IS SHORT,

wear your party pants.

LORETTA LAROCHE

Books, cats...
life is good.

Edward Gorey

If you have
a garden and
a library,
you have
everything
you need.

· ·

Marcus Tullius Cicero

I AM NOT AFRAID OF STORMS, FOR I AM LEARNING HOW TO SAIL MY SHIP.

Louisa May Alcott

FOLLOW YOUR INNER MOONLIGHT.

Allen Ginsberg

BLESSED ARE THEY WHO SEE BEAUTIFUL THINGS IN HUMBLE PLACES WHERE OTHER PEOPLE SEE NOTHING.

Camille Pissarro

HALF A LOAF IS BETTER THAN NONE.

JOHN HEYWOOD

Your Life,
no matter how bad
you think it is,
is Someone
else's Fairytale.

Wale Ayeni

It is impossible to

FEEL GRATEFUL

and depressed

IN THE

same MOMENT.

Naomi Williams

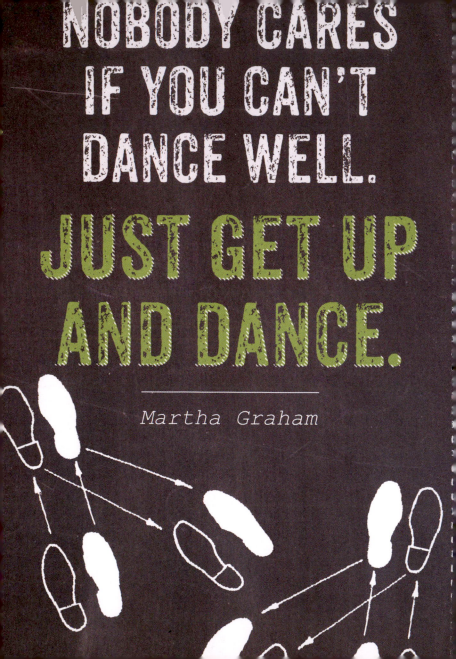

NOBODY CARES IF YOU CAN'T DANCE WELL.

JUST GET UP AND DANCE.

Martha Graham

I don't sing
because
I'm happy.
I'M HAPPY
because
I sing.

William James

DWELL ON THE BEAUTY OF LIFE. WATCH THE STARS, AND SEE YOURSELF RUNNING WITH THEM.

MARCUS AURELIUS

Write it on
your heart that
EVERY DAY
IS THE BEST
DAY
in the year.

Ralph Waldo Emerson

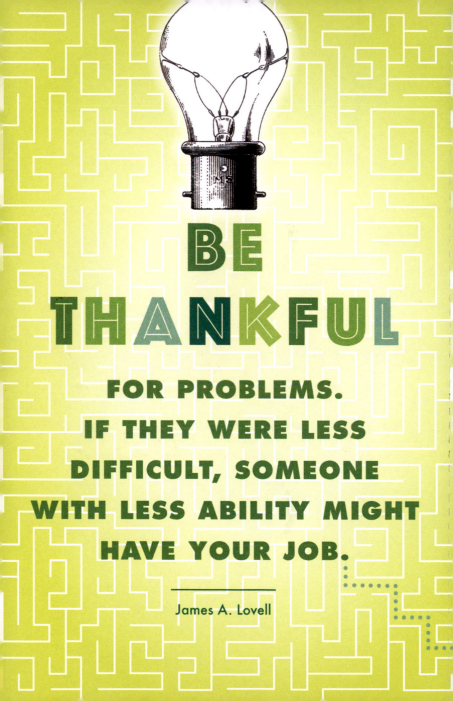

BE THANKFUL

FOR PROBLEMS.
IF THEY WERE LESS
DIFFICULT, SOMEONE
WITH LESS ABILITY MIGHT
HAVE YOUR JOB.

James A. Lovell

The time to be happy is now.

THE PLACE TO BE HAPPY IS HERE. THE WAY TO BE HAPPY IS TO MAKE OTHERS SO.

ROBERT G. INGERSOLL

SOMEONE IS **ENJOY**ING SHADE **TODAY** BECAUSE SOMEONE PLANTED A TREE A LONG TIME AGO.

WARREN BUFFETT

YOU'RE ALWAYS WITH YOURSELF, SO YOU MIGHT AS WELL ENJOY THE COMPANY.

DIANE VON FURSTENBERG

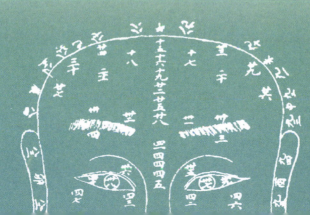

Your life is an occasion.

RISE

to it.

Suzanne Weyn

However vast
the darkness,
WE MUST SUPPLY
OUR OWN LIGHT.

Stanley Kubrick

When asked if my cup
is half-full or half-empty
my only response is that
I AM THANKFUL
I have a cup.

Sam Lefkowitz

Gratitude is
HAPPINESS
DOUBLED
by wonder.

G.K. Chesterton

When you
REALIZE
HOW PERFECT
EVERYTHING IS
you will tilt
your head back
and laugh at the sky.

———

Buddha

We pray for the big things and forget to **GIVE THANKS FOR** the ordinary, **SMALL GIFTS.**

Dietrich Bonhoeffer

NOW AND THEN
IT'S GOOD TO PAUSE
IN OUR PURSUIT OF
HAPPINESS AND

JUST
BE HAPPY.

GUILLAUME APOLLINAIRE

Be Grateful

to the people who
make us happy;
they are the charming
gardeners who make
our souls blossom.
_____

Marcel Proust

GRATITUDE IS **LOOKING ON THE BRIGHTER SIDE OF LIFE,** EVEN IF IT MEANS HURTING YOUR EYES.

ELLEN D GENERES

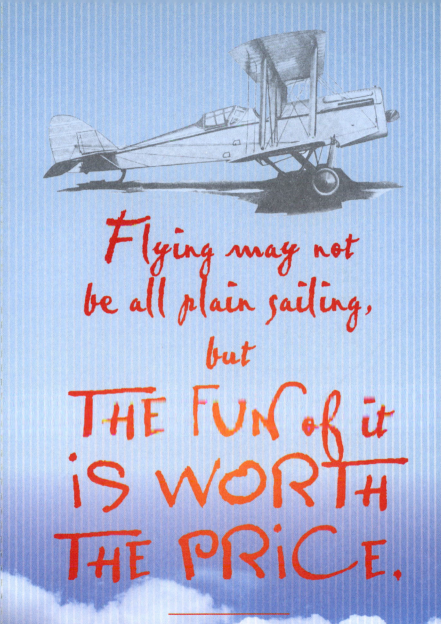

Flying may not
be all plain sailing,
but
THE FUN of it
IS WORTH
THE PRICE.

Amelia Earhart

My socks may not match, but my *feet* ARE ALWAYS WARM.

Maureen McCullough

THINGS TURN
OUT BEST FOR
PEOPLE WHO
**MAKE THE
BEST OF THE
WAY THINGS
TURN OUT.**

JOHN WOODEN

THIS A WONDERFUL DAY.

I'VE NEVER SEEN THIS ONE BEFORE.

MAYA ANGELOU

I'M
thankful to be
BREATHING,
on this side of the grass.
Whatever comes, comes.

Ron Perlman

ALL YOU NEED IS
FAITH, TRUST, AND A LITTLE
PIXIE DUST.

PETER PAN

What might seem to be

A SERIES OF UNFORTUNATE EVENTS MAY,

in fact,

BE THE FIRST STEPS OF A JOURNEY.

Lemony Snicket

GRATITUDE IS A CURRENCY

WE CAN SPEND WITHOUT FEAR OF BANKRUPTCY.

FRED DE WITT VAN AMBURGH

Every great dream BEGINs WITH A DREAMer.

Harriet Tubman

I have CHOSEn TO BE HAPPY because it is good for my health.

Voltaire

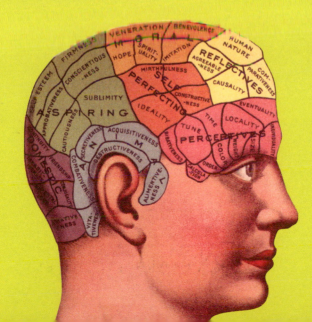

When you realize there is nothing lacking,

THE whole WORLD BELONGS TO YOU.

Lao Tzu

JOY IS WHAT HAPPENS WHEN WE ALLOW OURSELVES TO *Recognize how good things* REALLY *are.*

MARIANNE WILLIAMSON

THE ONLY PEOPLE WITH WHOM YOU SHOULD TRY TO GET EVEN ARE THOSE WHO HAVE HELPED YOU.

John E. Southard

I'm too grateful
to be hateful.
I am too **Blessed**
to be stressed.

———————

El DeBarge

CELEBRATE
what you want
MORE
of.

———————

Tom Peters

Those who
**BRING SUNSHINE
TO THE LIVES
OF OTHERS**
cannot keep it
from themselves.

James Matthew Barrie

DON'T SWEAT TOMORROW,
you haven't even met. Open your eyes to today.

Steve Maraboli

Let's all
TAKE A
MOMENT AND
BE THANKFUL
*that spiders
don't fly.*

———————

Unknown

EVERY MOMENT IS a FRESH beginning.

T.S. Eliot

I AM THANKFUL FOR LAUGHTER,

EXCEPT WHEN MILK COMES OUT OF MY NOSE.

WOODY ALLEN

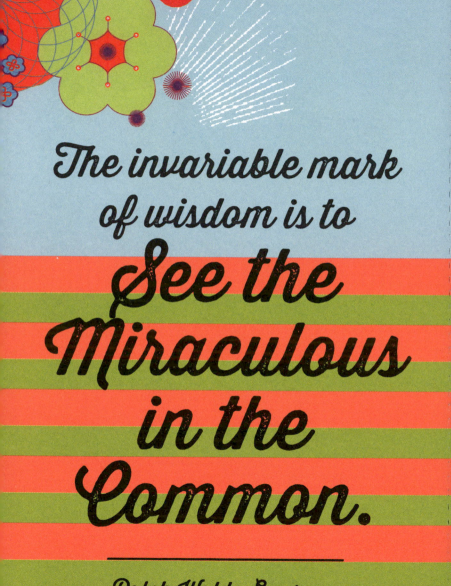

The invariable mark of wisdom is to See the Miraculous in the Common.

Ralph Waldo Emerson

Always
LOOK ON THE
BRIGHT SIDE
of life.
Otherwise
it'll be too
dark to read.

———————

Unknown

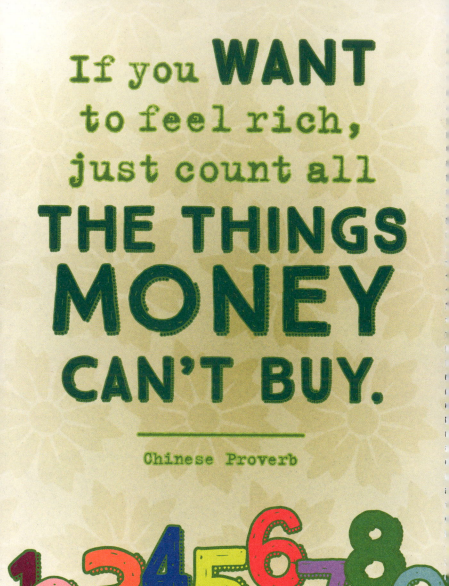

If you **WANT** to feel rich, just count all **THE THINGS MONEY CAN'T BUY.**

Chinese Proverb

CHERISH ALL YOUR HAPPY MOMENTS;

they make a fine cushion for old age.

Booth Tarkington

I am one of those people who just can't help GETting A KICK OUT OF LIFE, even when it's a kick in the teeth.

....

Polly Adler

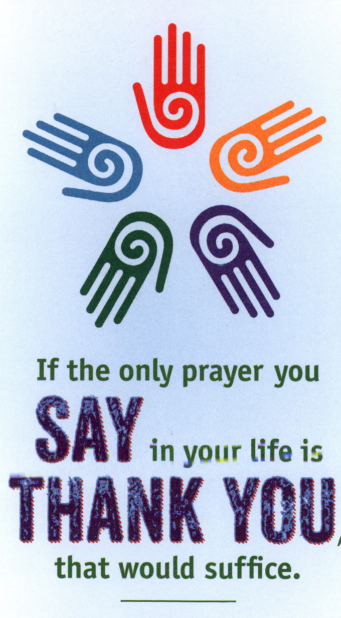

If the only prayer you
SAY in your life is
THANK YOU,
that would suffice.

—————

Meister Eckhart

Don't **GIVE** *up.*
Don't lose **HOPE.**
Don't sell out.

———————

Christopher Reeve

When the burdens of the presidency seem heavy, I always remind myself

IT COULD BE WORSE.

I could be a mayor.

Lyndon B. Johnson

THERE ARE
exactly as MANY
special OCCASIONS
IN LIFE *as we choose*
TO CELEBRATE.

Robert Brault

EARTH PROVIDES
enough to satisfy every man's needs, but not every man's greed.

Mahatma Gandhi

Prayers go up and
BLESSINGS
COME *down.*

Yiddish proverb

THANK YOU FOR the tragedy. I need it for my ART.

Kurt Cobain

Think about all
the things you
have to
BE THANKFUL
for...
AND SMILE.
The world will
smile with you.

———————

Frank Bettger

Today me will
LIVE IN
THE PRESENT,
unless it's unpleasant
in which case
me will eat a cookie.

....

Cookie Monster

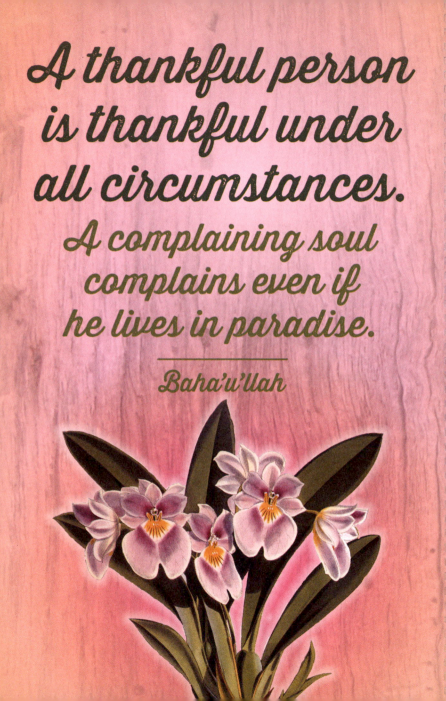

A thankful person is thankful under all circumstances. A complaining soul complains even if he lives in paradise.

Baha'u'llah

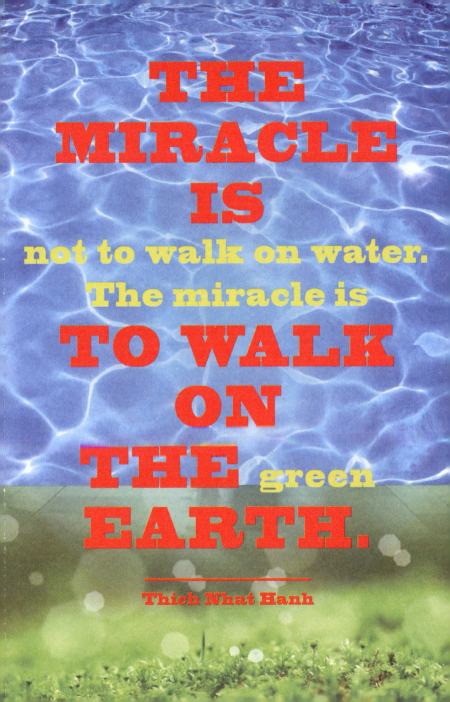

THE MIRACLE IS not to walk on water. The miracle is TO WALK ON THE green EARTH.

Thich Nhat Hanh

What we do for ourselves dies with us. What we

DO FOR OTHERS

and the world remains, and is immortal.

Albert Pike

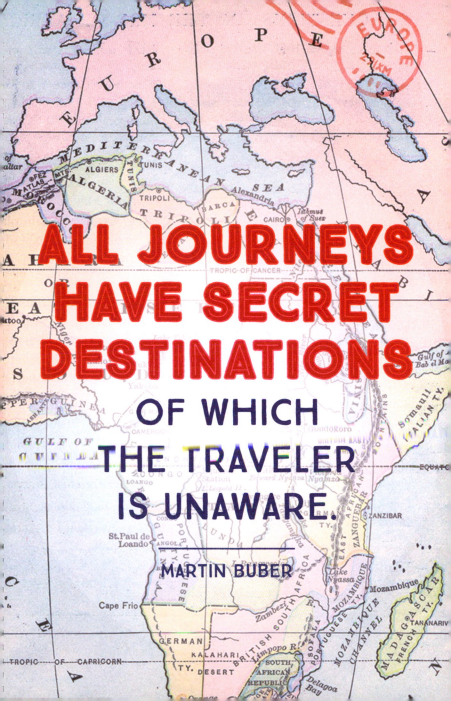

ALL JOURNEYS
HAVE SECRET
DESTINATIONS
OF WHICH
THE TRAVELER
IS UNAWARE.

MARTIN BUBER

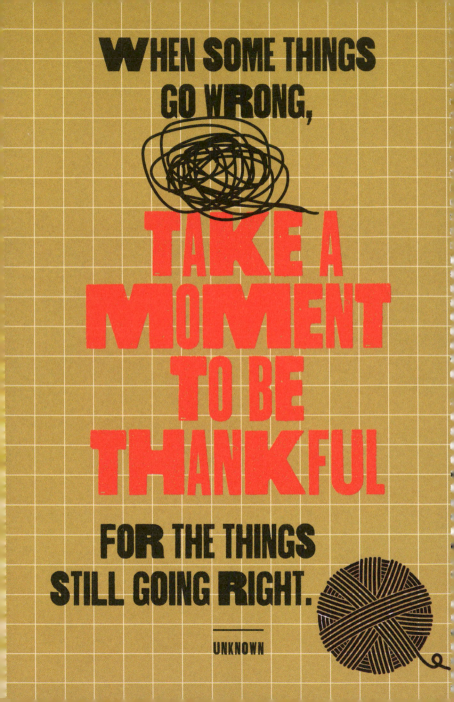

WHEN SOME THINGS GO WRONG, TAKE A MOMENT TO BE THANKFUL FOR THE THINGS STILL GOING RIGHT.

UNKNOWN

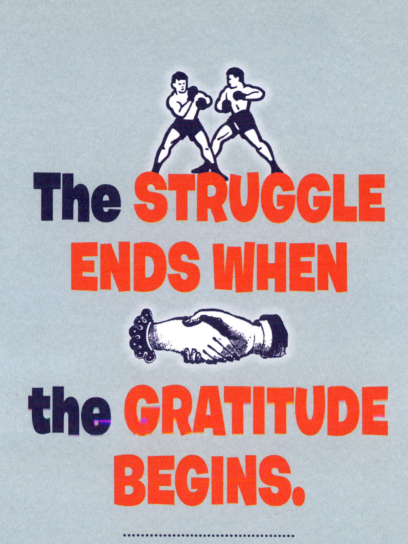

The STRUGGLE ENDS WHEN the GRATITUDE BEGINS.

Neale Donald Walsch

You live once and
LIFE IS WONDERFUL,
so eat the damned
red velvet cupcake.

—————

Emma Stone

Life isn't about how to survive in the storm. It's about how to

DANCE IN THE RAIN.

Taylor Swift

I like to
SEE THE
GLASS AS
HALF FULL...
hopefully of
Jack Daniels.

Darynda Jones

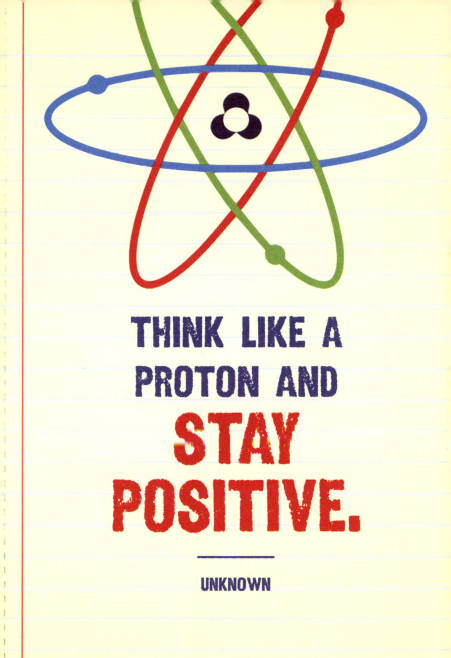

THINK LIKE A
PROTON AND
STAY
POSITIVE.

UNKNOWN

A MAN IS HAPPY SO LONG AS HE CHOOSEs TO BE HAPPY.

Aleksandr Solzhenitsyn

LEARNING IS A GIFT.

EVEN WHEN PAIN IS YOUR TEACHER.

MAYA WATSON

Time is precious.

WASTE IT WISELY.

K. Bromberg

ENJOY LIFE.

There's plenty of time to be dead.

———————

Hans Christian Andersen

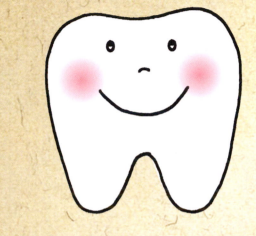

LIFE IS SHORT.
SMILE
WHILE YOU STILL
HAVE TEETH.

MALLORY HOPKINS

WORRY
is like rocking
in a rocking chair.
It gives you something
to do, but
**NEVER GETS YOU
ANYWHERE.**

———————

Erma Bombeck

8   9   10   11   12
15   16   17   18   19   7
23   24   25   26

DON'T COUNT THE DAYS,

MAKE
THE DAYS
COUNT.

MUHAMMAD ALI

As you SLIDE DOWN THE BANISTERS OF LIFE, may the splinters never point in the wrong direction.

Irish proverb

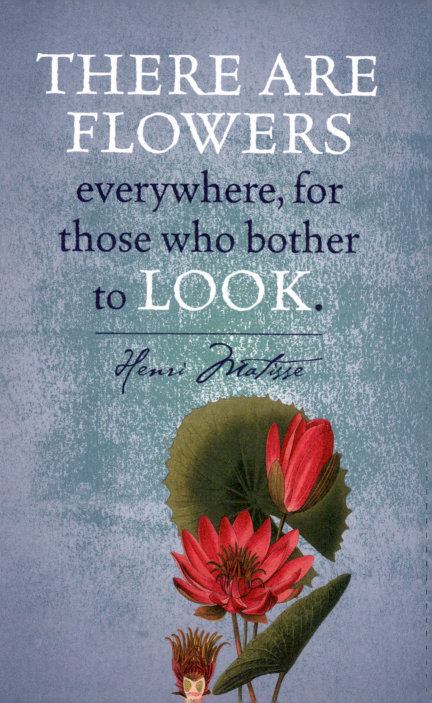

THERE ARE
FLOWERS
everywhere, for
those who bother
to LOOK.

Henri Matisse

Act happy, feel happy,
BE HAPPY,
WITHOUT
A REASON
in the world.

———————

Dan Millman

GIVE THANKS
FOR UNKNOWN
BLESSINGS
already on their way.

Native American Saying

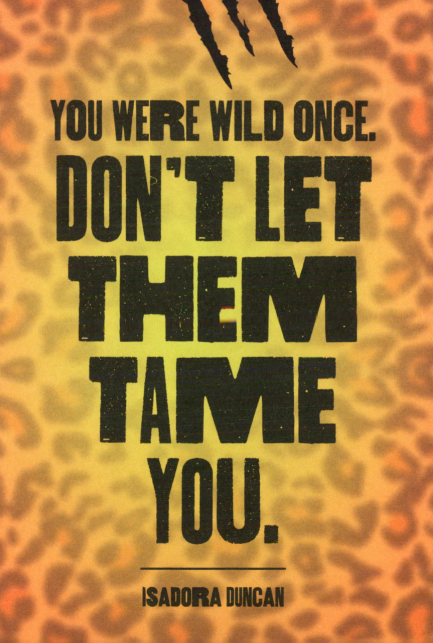

YOU WE**R**E WILD ONCE.
DON'T LET
THEM
TA**M**E
YOU.

ISADO**R**A DUNCAN

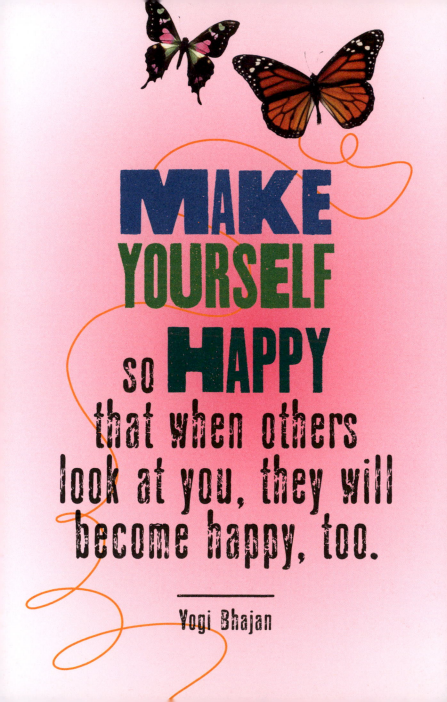

MAKE YOURSELF HAPPY so that when others look at you, they will become happy, too.

— Yogi Bhajan

Wine is constant proof that

GOD

loves us and

LOVES
TO SEE
US HAPPY.

Benjamin Franklin

IT IS NOT ENOUGH TO KNOW HOW TO RIDE, YOU MUST ALSO KNOW HOW TO FALL.

MEXICAN PROVERB

You could get hit by a bus
tomorrow, so you'd better

be at peace

with whatever you
got going at the moment.

———————

Joseph Gordon-Levitt

LOOK UPON THE BRIGHT SIDE OF LIFE,

GATHERING ITS ROSES AND SUNSHINE AND MAKING THE MOST THAT HAPPENS SEEMS THE BEST.

— Dorothy Dix

TO **FLY**,
WE HAVE TO
HAVE RESISTANCE.

———

MAYA LIN

SPECIAL HANDLING

FRAGILE
HANDLE WITH CARE

THE BEST THINGS IN LIFE ARE FREE

(PLUS SHIPPING AND HANDLING).

UNKNOWN

VIA AIR MAIL

Children have neither past nor future; they **ENJOY THE PRESENT,** which very few of us do.

Jean de la Bruyere

TO
MOVE A
MOUNTAIN,
BEGIN BY CARRYING
AWAY SMALL
STONES.

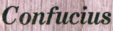

Confucius

BE GLAD OF LIFE BECAUSE
IT GIVES YOU THE CHANCE
TO **LOVE**
AND TO WORK AND TO
PLAY AND
TO
LOOK AT
THE STARS.

HENRY VAN DYKE

Be not afraid

of going slowly.
Be afraid of
standing still.

———————

Chinese proverb

EACH DAY COMES BEARING ITS OWN GIFTS.

Untie the ribbons.

Ruth Ann Schabacker

We're so busy watching out for what's just ahead of us that we don't

TAKE TIME
TO ENJOY

where we are.

Bill Watterson

FOR EVERY DARK NIGHT, THERE'S A BRIGHTER DAY.

— TUPAC

THINK BIG
THOUGHTS. BUT
RELISH SMALL
TREASURES.

H. Jackson Brown Jr.

FOR EVERY MINUTE

YOU ARE ANGRY
YOU LOSE

60 SECONDS
OF HAPPINESS.

RALPH WALDO EMERSON

TO CREATE ONE'S OWN WORLD TAKES
Courage.

GEORGIA O'KEEFE

LEARN FROM the MISTAKES of others. You can never live long enough to make them all yourself.

Groucho Marx

A
BEAUTIFUL
thing
IS NEVER
PERFECT.

Egyptian proverb

DREAM

The future belongs
to those who
**BELIEVE
IN THE
BEAUTY
OF** their
DREAMS.

Eleanor Roosevelt

Stamens 2138-MN
a Petals; b Stamens; c
Ovary; d Style; e Stigma

LIFE IS NOT ABOUT HAVING EVERYTHING. IT'S ABOUT **FIND**ING **MEANING IN EVERYTHING.**

- - - - - - - - - - - - - - - - - -

Joel Randymar

Do not dwell
in the past,
do not dream
of the future;

CONCENTRATE

the mind

ON THE PRESENT

moment.

———————

Buddha

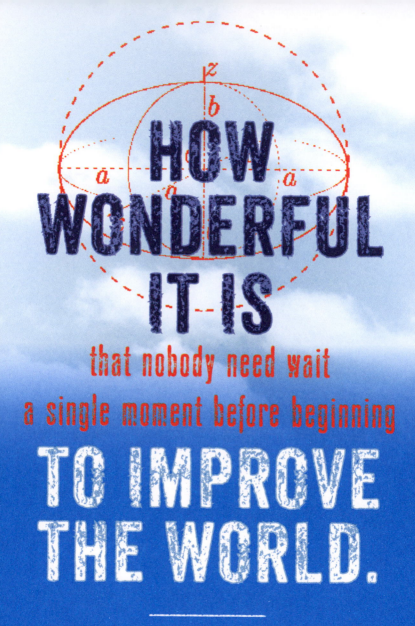

HOW WONDERFUL IT IS

that nobody need wait a single moment before beginning

TO IMPROVE THE WORLD.

ANNE FRANK

BE *present in all things and* THANKFUL FOR ALL THINGS.

Maya Angelou

NEVER GIVE UP,

for that is just the place and time that the tide will turn.

———————————

Harriet Beecher Stowe

TREASURE
the
LOVE

*you receive above all.
It will survive long after
your gold and good health
have vanished.*

———————

Og Mandino

GOD GAVE US
OUR RELATIVES;
THANK GOD
WE CAN
CHOOSE
OUR FRIENDS.

———————————

ETHEL WATTS MUMFORD

GRACE ISN'T
A LITTLE PRAYER YOU CHANT BEFORE RECEIVING A MEAL. IT'S
A WAY TO LIVE.

JACQUELINE WINSPEAR

IT IS NOTJOY THAT
MAKES US GRATEFUL.
IT IS
GRATITUDE
THAT MAKES
US JOYFUL.

DAVID RAST

If you don't think

EVERY DAY IS A GOOD DAY,

just try missing one.

———————

Cavett Robert

Keep your
FACE to THE
SUNSHINE
and you cannot
see the shadows.

———————

Helen Keller

LIVE
THE ACTUAL
MOMENT. ONLY
THIS
MOMENT
IS LIFE.

THICH NHAT HAHN

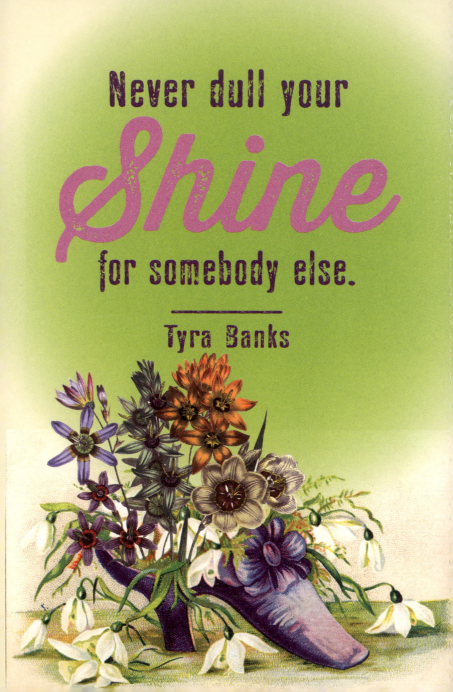

Never dull your *Shine* for somebody else.

— Tyra Banks

SINCE WE CANNOT GET WHAT WE LIKE, LET US LIKE WHAT WE CAN GET.

SPANISH PROVERB

IF YOU NEED
SOMETHING TO

BE
GRATEFUL
FOR, CHECK
YOUR PULSE.

AMERICAN PROVERB

Don't postpone joy until you have learned all of your lessons.

JOY IS YOUR LESSON.

— ALAN COHEN

If you're feeling helpless,

HELP SOMEONE.

Aung San Suu Kyi

The clearest
sign of

WISDOM

IS

continued

CHEERFULNESS.

Michel Montaigne

If you see
no reason to
GIVE
THANKS,
the fault lies
in yourself.

Tecumseh

THINK OF ALL THE BEAUTY THAT IS

STILL LEFT IN AND AROUND YOU AND BE HAPPY.

———

ANNE FRANK

The dry seasons
in life do not last.
The rains
will come
again.

Sarah Ban Breathnach

THE FOOLISH MAN

SEEKs
HAPPINESS

IN THE DISTANCE,
THE WISE GROWS IT
UNDER HIS FEET.

JAMES OPPENHEIM

THERE ARE
far, far BETTER
THINGS
AHEAD
than any we
leave behind.

———————

C.S. Lewis

Keep

a green tree in your heart and perhaps a

Singing

bird will come.

———————————

Chinese proverb

You know
IT WAS A
GOOD DAY
*if you didn't hit
or bite anyone.*

Nathaniel, age 4

You won't
BE HAPPY
with more until
you're happy
WITH WHAT
YOU'VE GOT.

Viki King

THE BEST THING
ONE CAN DO WHEN
IT IS
RAINING IS TO

LET IT RAIN.

HENRY WADSWORTH LONGFELLOW